4-20

A BOOK OF CHINESE FESTIVALS

Judith Karen Gee

Illustrated by Chen Zhi Huang

Canadian Cataloguing in Publication Data

Gee, Judith Karen, 1950-
  A book of Chinese festivals

  ISBN 0-9692499-4-2

  1. Festivals - China - Juvenile literature.
I. Huang, Chen-zhi. II. Title.
GT4883.A2G43 1989   j394.2'6951   C89-091170-3

Printed in Canada by

Friesen Printers
a Division of D. W. Friesen & Sons Ltd.
Altona, Manitoba R0G 0B0
Canada

ACKNOWLEDGEMENTS

To all the students and teachers of the University of Science and Technology who provided me with information on Chinese festivals and to Marie-Luise Latsch whose book introduced me to a more detailed look at Chinese festivals.

DEDICATION

To Michael

INTRODUCTION

So many times, books are written for older students and adults, and books about a country's holidays are no exception. During my stay in China I found books about China's festivals but none that children could enjoy. In this book of Chinese festivals I describe just a few traditional festivals celebrated in China today. These festivals or holidays are practised mainly by the *Han* nationality.

Judith Karen Gee

SPRING FESTIVAL (*CHUN JIE*) OR CHINESE LUNAR NEW YEAR

Spring festival is the most popular festival in China as Christmas is in the western world. This holiday usually occurs in late January or early February according to the lunar calendar.

The Chinese New Year is a time for family get-togethers, a time to visit friends, a rest from work, time for parties and programs, and a time to begin afresh. The Chinese believe that this is the time of the year that all bills should be paid. There is also hope for better things in the coming year.

		1989	FEBRUARY	1989		
SUN	MON	TUE	WED	THU	FRI	SAT
			1	2	3	4
5	**6**	7	8	9	10	11
12	13	14	15	16	17	18
19	20	21	22	23	24	25
26	27	28				

SPRING FESTIVAL CUSTOMS

New Year's pictures which have been made for 2,000 years still decorate homes today. The pictures are usually of ancient heroes or symbols of good luck which are put on either side of the door of the houses for protection. The pictures that guard the door are sometimes guardians of the gate, kitchen gods, plump children with fish, peonies, peaches, goldfish, phoenixes, themes from Chinese opera and pictures from myths. Sometimes strips of red paper are hung by doorways. Short poems in the form of couplets express wishes for good luck. For example, one couplet may read, "May all your wishes be fulfilled".

In North China families burn yellow paper (special for burning) as money. This is done for dead relatives so that they can have money in the other world. The money must be burned before midnight.

Also in North China, a popular folk dance called *Yangko* is performed on the third day of the Spring Festival.

"a plump child with fish"

SPRING FESTIVAL PRESENTS

Many relatives and friends exchange gifts at this time. Since eating and drinking are very important, people favour giving food items as presents. Cakes, candies and dried fruits are the favourites. For the adults, cigarettes, wine and tea are often exchanged. Children, single adults and newlyweds will often get money in a red envelope along with toys and new clothes for the children and furniture for the newlyweds. "Lucky money", however, is traditionally given by married people to single members of the family or friends who visit during Chinese New Year.

"Lucky" money is given in a red envelope.

SPRING FESTIVAL FOOD

Food is usually prepared before the holiday. In the southern part of China the favourite and most popular dishes are *nian gao* (sweet steamed glutinous rice pudding) and *zong zi* (leaf wrapped glutinous rice balls with many kinds of fillings).

In northern China the main dishes are *man tou* (steamed white bread) and meat dumplings, usually pork, known as *baozi* or *jiaozi*. Of course, other meats such as duck, chicken, fish, lamb and beef are eaten during this holiday.

Baozi and *jiaozi* are popular main dishes in northern and southern China.

NEW YEAR'S EVE AND NEW YEAR'S DAY

This is the time the family is together, and this is when they exchange presents. Then comes a large dinner when the best of everything is put on the table. A number of families put a whole fish on the table to symbolize unity. Later, many families will watch special programs on television until midnight.

At midnight firecrackers and fireworks of every kind will be set off. This may last for an hour or more.

New Year's day is a time for eating and for visiting relatives and friends. Since many Chinese in recent years have been able to afford telephones, much of the visiting of friends has decreased. Best wishes for a prosperous and lucky new year can be said over the telephone instead of in person.

Firecrackers and fireworks are set off before midnight of the new year.

THE LANTERN FESTIVAL - *YUAN XIAO JIE*

The Lantern Festival is celebrated on the 15th day of the first lunar month. It is a traditional Chinese celebration when people eat flavoured dumplings and enjoy displays of coloured lanterns some placed on either side of the doorway of the houses.

Chinese scholars are still arguing about when this holiday started. The lanterns date back as far as the Western *Zhou* Dynasty between the 16th and 17th centuries AD. The festival itself dates back to the *Han* Dynasty (206 - 220 AD). The modern day lantern festival began in the *T'ang* Dynasty (618 - 907 AD). But no matter when this festival began it is celebrated today with bright lanterns and fireworks.

Since the *Han* Dynasty, on every Lantern Festival day, some people light lamps to pray to spirits for good health and good fortune.

Since the *Song* Dynasty, on Lantern Festival day, people also eat *yuan xiao*, a kind of sticky rice, always sweet, together with sugar and other delicious foods such as almonds, orange peel, and bean paste.

In rural areas children play "hide and seek" with lanterns during the Lantern Festival.

Children are playing hide and seek with lanterns.

Stilt walkers are a traditional folk activity.

The lion dance is the most loved by Chinese people.

LANTERN FESTIVAL CUSTOMS

Like so many Chinese festivals, there are customs that go along with the lantern festival. There are various traditional folk activities such as stilt walking, dragon and lion boat races, donkey dances, waist drums, folk dances and, of course, eating.

The custom of eating dumplings on the day of Lantern Festival has been passed along from generation to generation since the *T'ang* Dynasty (618 - 907 AD).

Perhaps the most popular of traditional folk activities are the stilt walkers and the dragon and lion dances. The stilt walkers are groups of men, some with false beards and painted faces, others disguised as women, dancing around with a rather funny gait.

The lion dance is the most loved by Chinese people. One man operates the wooden head and another the back. The dance called "The Game of the Lion" was supposed to scare away devils. Now, this dance is often seen at an acrobatic performance in a theatre. But there are still performances held in city parks, while in the country troupes of lion dancers parade through village streets.

No Lantern Festival would be complete without lanterns. Some families light as many lanterns as there are family members. If a family wants more children, they show this by lighting extra lanterns. Of course, with the one-child family policy in China this practice is limited to the rural areas and minority nationalities. Some also use the lantern during the festival to light the way to visit a neighbour.

Some families light as many lanterns as there are family members.

THE DRAGON BOAT FESTIVAL

The Dragon Boat Festival usually occurs in the months of June or July when the weather is the hottest. This festival was originally celebrated to serve the river god. People thought that the rivers were controlled by a dragon which decided where the rain would fall.

Later, this festival was celebrated in remembrance of *Qu Yuan*, a great poet and loyal figure of the state. Many unfortunate incidents in *Qu Yuan's* state caused him to jump into the river, thus giving his life for his country. Many people respected *Qu Yuan* and rowed out into the river to search for his body. But alas, they could not find it. Since that time, dragon boat racing has been held every year on the fifth day of the fifth month of the lunar calendar.

The Dragon Boat Festival is celebrated to serve the dragon river god.

DRAGON BOAT FESTIVAL FOOD

What festival wouldn't be complete without food? As with all Chinese festivals food is a popular item. During the Dragon Boat Festival, the preparation and eating of *zong zi* (leaf-wrapped glutinous rice balls with many kinds of filling) is widespread. This custom is also linked with *Qu Yuan's* death. To honour him, people threw *zong zi* into the river. The eating of *zong zi* has become even more popular today.

Qu Yuan, the great poet, gave his life for his country.

DRAGON BOAT FESTIVAL CUSTOMS

Dragon boat racing is said to have occurred even before *Qu Yuan's* death, as early as 770 - 476 BC. It is said that a certain king used boat races to train his navy. This festival became well known during the *T'ang* Dynasty (618 - 907 AD) especially in the south of China.

The dragon boats are very narrow and their length can be up to 30 metres. Of course, each boat has a carved dragon head at the prow. Each boat carries eight to 15 pairs of oarsmen. When the race begins, two men in the middle of the boat beat a drum and a gong. A man at the front of the boat waves a flag and chants to regulate the strokes of the rowers.

These Dragon Boat Festival activities are much less celebrated than in the past, but during the Dragon Year many contests are held and traditions renewed.

Each dragon boat carries eight to fifteen pairs of oarsmen.

MID-AUTUMN OR MOON FESTIVAL

Mid-Autumn Festival falls on the 15th day of the eighth lunar month, usually August or September. The celebration of this festival is based on popular Chinese legends. There are several, but the one about *Chang E* is most famous.

It is said that *Chang E's* husband *Hou Yi* was asked by the emperor to shoot extra suns that had appeared in the sky which were causing heat and drought in the land. This he did with his magic bow and arrows. Because of this, *Hou Yi* became famous and was called to the fairy palace of the Queen Mother of the West. He was rewarded with a pill of immortality. But he was to prepare himself through fasting and praying before taking the pill. He began his task but was called away on business, so he hid the pill.

While he was away, his wife *Chang E* noticed a light and sweet odour coming from the place he had hidden it. She could not resist temptation and ate the pill. At that moment she could fly! Upon his return, her husband *Hou Yi* chased her, but alas he could not catch *Chang E* because she flew all the way to the moon.

She was breathing so hard that the pill fell out of her mouth turning into a jade rabbit, and she turned into a three-legged toad. Ever since then she has lived on the moon and her husband built a palace in the sun so that they could see each other on the 15th of each month.

Hou Yi is shooting extra suns in the sky.

MOON FESTIVAL CUSTOMS

Moon cakes go on sale just before festival time. They have many different fillings such as sugar, almonds, orange peel, bits of ham or beef, and bean paste.

The Moon Festival today is an ordinary workday, but families gather to have a special evening meal and visit friends and relatives. Together they watch the moon and eat moon cakes.

Families are watching the moon and eating moon cakes.

GLOSSARY

Chinese Vocabulary

baozi (boudse) : meat dumplings

Chang E (Chong Uh)

Chun jie (Chun jye)

Han (Hon) - nationality of most mainland Chinese

Hou Yi (Hou Yee)

jiaozi (jioudse) - meat dumplings

mantou (man tou) - steamed white bread

nian gao (nean gou) - sweet steamed glutinous rice pudding

Qu Yuan (Chu Uon) - a great poet and loyal servant to his country

Song (Sung)

Tang (Tang)

Yangko (Yangko) - folk dance in northern China

yuan xiao (uon sheou) - a sticky kind of rice

Yuan Xiao Jie (uon sheou jye) - Lantern Festival

Zhou (joe)

zong zi (dsung dse) - leaf-wrapped glutinous rice balls with many kinds of fillings

English Vocabulary

acrobatic (adj) - a person who is highly skilled in tumbling or trapeze performance is considered acrobatic.

celebration (n) - praise and honouring; observing a festival or event.

gait (n) - walk

immortality (n) - live forever

lunar (adj) - of the moon. The Chinese New Year begins according to the lunar calendar.

minority (n) - a group within a country which differs in race, religion or from the dominant group (such as the Han in China).

phoenix (n) - an important mythical bird symbolizing long life in Chinese culture.

prosperous (adj) - doing well.

symbolize (v) - to stand for.

traditionally (adv) - handing down of beliefs, customs, stories from parents to children.

troupe (n) - a company or band of actors of dancers.